INTRODUCTION

For anyone who seeks to make sense of a place like San Francisco, its tensions and triumphs and compulsive appeal, I have a suggestion that might not be obvious: look hard at the buildings and structures that line its streets and climb its hills, that nestle close to the water or intrude upon your view.

The best of the structures around us are architectural gems to be sure, from individual modern landmarks to collections of atmospheric treats à la the Painted Ladies of Alamo Square. But the structures that frame them in the background are equally important, combining into tapestries threaded with the politics, architectural fads, and cultural values of the eras in which they were conceived. They're not simply the top layer of a peninsula at the edge of continent. They are essential to San Francisco's story. They are signposts, or translations, and they help bring this complex and often contested city into sharper focus.

That is the aim of this book: a nudge to see the familiar in fresh ways, reading the urban landscape to glean all that it reveals. A bit of surface decoration can be explained by long-ago events; small details can tip the balance in terms of whether a structure is dynamic or drab. This is true from a variety of perspectives, as I attempt to show with the fifty structures and four sections that follow. The first section, "Towers," goes beyond questions of height to look at how different eras of the city have expressed themselves by the structures they placed on the skyline. "Connections" explores how individual structures are part of larger patterns and networks, strands within webs that might be obvious but often are not. The section called "Clues" shows the range of ways in which architecture can hint at something much larger, from shifting neighborhood demographics to the demise of a once-imposing freeway. Finally, "Waterfront" is a ten-stop journey along the peninsula's edge, west to east, the defining edge and culmination of the inland city.

This is my second *Cityscapes* collection. As with the first, I've drawn from fifty structures—some of them instantly recognizable, some of them obscure—that first appeared in my weekly column of words and photographs in the *San Francisco Chronicle*. But what you'll encounter here differs substantially from what first appeared in print. The text has been revised and expanded, since chapters that once were monologues are now part of a larger chorus. And many of the photographs are new, a response to the reality of a city where it sometimes seems that building cranes outnumber artisanal coffee shops. San Francisco is a place where landscapes are ever in transition; a photograph from twenty-four or thirty-six months ago can seem like an artifact of ancient times. What doesn't change is the sense that this is a city filled with vivid surprise—a compact world waiting to be explored, on foot and with ever more discerning eyes.

San Francisco is defined by its hills and its shore, the sharp blue sky and the shifting blue ocean and bay. It is also defined by its tall buildings, the built terrain that emerges from what nature gave us.

If this notion sounds heretical, consider: Even Herb Caen, who for decades was the arbiter of the city's values as a *San Francisco Chronicle* newspaper columnist, in his 1948 book *Baghdad by the Bay* gave an approving nod to "the imposing bristle of skyscrapers…arranged just so in just the right place, to look like a city should look."

The skyline has changed mightily since then—the once-maligned Transamerica Pyramid is an internationally known symbol of the city, for starters—and the bristle is more imposing. Many people don't like it, but there is much of architectural value in our high-rises. If nothing else, the peaks and rough edges make plain that the task facing twenty-first-century San Francisco is not new: to evolve as a global city, but still feel like home.

TOWERS

Russ Building

235 Montgomery Street

When Herb Caen praised his "just so" skyline, this 435-feet peak marked
the summit of the Financial District. Since then, more than thirty towers
have climbed past it, but in terms of sheer drama this remains the
aesthetic peak. It's also the embodiment of Jazz Age romance, a full
block of ornate Gothic-flavored masonry that ascends in jagged stages
from Montgomery Street with a leap and then a scramble to a central
crown. What's being celebrated is a city on the rise, radiant and brash,
each upward nip and tuck a show in itself. Planners since then have
required other buildings to step back as they soar—but in comparison
to this they are diagrams, and they lack the driving force.

George Kelham, 32 floors, 1927

Saints Peter and Paul Church

666 Filbert Street

Before the age of skyscrapers, churches were often the tallest buildings around, visual anchors as well as affirmations of faith. This still holds true in neighborhoods such as the historic Italian enclave North Beach, which is hard to imagine without this center of Catholic worship. A disciplined but joyous proclamation of majesty no matter your beliefs, it is visible from afar and memorable up close with its folds of mystically intricate stonework that stab the heavens with down-to-earth delights. Washington Square is a beloved oasis, the wooded crossroads of North Beach; without this consecrated cliff as a backdrop, in some ways it would be just another patch of green. *Charles Fantoni, 191 feet, 1924*

Clocktower Lofts

461 Second Street

Here is another tower that serves as a marker, this one not by intent but by chance. The former home of Schmidt Lithograph began life three stories high, the lone flourish a procession of arched upper-floor windows. Then came the Campanile-like addition, a container for elevator machinery and water tanks adorned by a large clock on each side. Sixteen years later, the Bay Bridge opened, touching down alongside the block. This gave the slender shaft a regional prominence that did not diminish as printing presses were replaced by residential lofts, and now as the much taller spikes of downtown's residential skyline draw near. Despite all these changes it still announces the time, and still tells you where you are. *H. C. Baumann, 3 stories with 170-foot tower, 1907 and 1920; conversion to lofts by David Baker Architects, 1992*

Sutro Tower

1 La Avanzada Street

The most prominent marker of all is this broadcasting tower that begins
834 feet above sea level and transmitted its first signals on July 4,
1973—and ever since then has stood as a lightning rod that shows how
subjective something like architectural judgment can be. Many of us see
a skeletal robot that mars the wooded slopes, the orange-and-white-
striped paint scheme the final insult. From another perspective, the
three-legged creation is a symbol of home every bit as potent as Twin
Peaks. This may explain why Sutro Tower has achieved cult status among
younger city dwellers. It makes no pretense to be anything except what
it is; in an age and a city where authenticity is in demand, perhaps that
is enough. *A. C. Martin Partners, 977 feet, 1973*

Whittell Building

166 Geary Street

Beyond inches and feet a tower can be measured by its aspirational spirit, which is why this diminutive upstart commands attention just east of Union Square. It was under construction when the 1906 earthquake hit, and its steel frame on a deep foundation stood tall while the blocks around it collapsed or burned. There was talk of completing it with fireproof steel walls before workers switched to brown brick above terra cotta, with a pert cap to top things off. The emphatic verticality gives the building an upward punch unlike anything nearby, be it Union Square's stone-clad Beaux Arts landmarks or the shoebox blur of later hotel towers. Because of this setting, our spirited survivor stands out all the more.

Shea and Shea, 16 stories, 1906

Carillon Tower

1100 Gough Street

This bulbous white-concrete shaft dates from the early 1960s, the era of unfettered urban renewal, with futuristic Saint Mary's Cathedral to the west and the housing projects of the Western Addition among its neighbors to the south. It occupies a block by itself with a design that belongs in a beachside resort more than a close-packed city. The incongruity should be jarring—yet on sunny days the curvaceous form has an eye-catching swing, the upward motion accented by zipper-like stacks of balconies, a cloud-high oasis offering a privileged take on the city below. Many towers radiate self-importance. This one just wants its residents to enjoy life and savor the views, and who can argue with that? *Donald Powers Smith, 19 stories, 1964*

580 California Street

In the 1980s, when the ideal was for new buildings to look old, architect Philip Johnson turned skyscraper design into a parade of visual stunts. For a site across from the fifty-two-story tower that once housed Bank of America's headquarters, his hook was to run shallow bays from a tall arcade up granite walls and conclude with twelve cloaked, faceless figures against a mansard roof of dark glass. The rounded bays and regal summit are an outsider's nod to Victoriana; Johnson privately likened the statues to the Board of Supervisors and the mayor. Mischievous, perhaps, but effective: a crowd-pleasing show that continues to outshine its buttoned-down neighbors. *Johnson/Burgee Architects, statues by Muriel Castanis, 23 stories, 1984*

Hunter-Dulin Building

111 Sutter Street

Equally idiosyncratic is this French chateau at skyline scale, brought to us by the New York architects who designed that city's Waldorf Astoria Hotel (and where, so goes the legend, Sam Spade had his office). It begins with a deep, vaulted entrance and a base that culminates in a line of medallions decorated with mythical beasts. The terra cotta–clad shaft is topped by fastidious arches. The cornice sprouts eagles, and the show concludes with a thirty-eight-foot-tall gabled roof adorned with twenty copper spires. What looks elegant in the sky is exotic on the ground: towers once lived this dual life as a matter of course, rewarding in different dimensions, and it would be good for all of us if they did so again.

Schultze and Weaver, 25 stories, 1926

44 Montgomery Street

Across from the Hunter Dulin Building is San Francisco's most unapologetically modern tower, a crisp metal monolith that treated its masonry neighbors as a backdrop against which the New could proclaim that Today had Arrived. But the artistic ambitions are real, as is the clarity with which they were pursued. Dark marble columns two stories high line the sidewalk beneath aluminum bands that stretch straight to the heavens. The metalwork is twice as dense at the bottom and top—marking the base below, the cornice above—in a gesture to architectural order that only a design buff would discern. The quest was to dazzle the eye. In the right light, like it or not, success cannot be denied.

John Graham, 43 stories, 1966

Embarcadero Center

Battery Street to the Embarcadero, between Clay and
Sacramento Streets

An even more determined proclamation of changing times was John
Portman's quartet of slit-windowed concrete office buildings linked
by sidewalks in the sky, purposefully set apart from a city that favors
street life and small blocks. But as so often happens, time's passage has
turned shock into a shrug. What once was mocked as a set of upright
bundles of computer punch cards now endures as a striking ensemble
on the skyline, a corporate enclave forged with an eye to maximum
impact from afar. Broad cliffs when viewed from the north or south, the
outcrops can seem impossibly thin when viewed from the east or west.
And from any angle, the complex demonstrates how quickly "the future"
can seem quaint. *John Portman, 30–45 stories, 1967–1983*

PORT OF

400 California Street

People who dislike modern architecture point to the 1960s as proof that its creators cared nothing about what had come before. Yet diligent architects have always sought to treat the surroundings with respect, even if their notion of "contextual design" differed from ours. Here, a thick high-rise was attached to a classical banking hall in a way that might now look awkward. But the fusion is one of restraint: the blunt tower stands slightly behind its grand neighbor, paneled in concrete with vertical ridges meant to evoke the fluted granite columns of the bank. The pairing exudes deference and warmth and architecture's ability to reach across generations with a steady hand, no matter the styles involved. *Banking hall: Bliss & Faville, 1908; tower: Anshen & Allen, 21 stories, 1967*

560 Mission Street

Glass is all the rage these days for architects and developers who want to brand their buildings with a contemporary sheen. The hard part is to convey something beyond the novelty of now—a challenge met here by Cesar Pelli with a broad box clad in smoky gray-green glass amid a cross-thatch of thin bands of aluminum painted forest green. What sounds dull and dark is luminous in person, clean layer upon layer, as captivating as the Japanese lamps cited by the architect as an inspiration. Pelli's firm has since designed the Salesforce Tower that will replace the Transamerica Pyramid as the city's tallest building; the real feat will be if the newcomer measures up to its relative nearby.

Pelli Clarke Pelli, 31 stories, 2002

700 Steiner Street

In the 1920s, before the notion of tall buildings became taboo in many parts of San Francisco, a sophisticated urbanism flourished in which then-new apartments rose above their neighbors with such civility that it was hard to take offense. Certainly that's the case on Alamo Square, where the Painted Ladies of the Victorian era outshine the relatively tall thirty-six-unit neighbor that followed them onto the scene by thirty years. But the orderly stucco mass with its patterned vertical bays and prim exterior fire escape should not be ignored by the picture-taking tourists who stop by. Dignified, dense, it reminds us that yesterday's city found ways to grow, and grow up, while staying true to itself.

Philip Harris, 6-plus stories, 1927

Coit Tower

1 Telegraph Hill Boulevard

If *icon* is a word too easily abused, it rings true when applied to the artful concrete cone at the top of Telegraph Hill. The tower that resulted from Lillie Hitchcock Coit's $100,000 bequest to city is both a grand finale to nature's summit and a restrained tonic to the surrounding patchwork of roofs, walls, flowers, and trees. Up it goes in a single strong stroke, solid walls and open peak, making certain that the fabled hill will remain prominent no matter what happens to the skyline beyond. Consider the proportions as well: the original design was half as tall as what we now revere. There are places in a city where extra height is the right response—including, sometimes, at the very top of a hill.

Arthur Brown Jr., 210 feet, 1934

If some structures reach to the heavens, others bind us more closely to each other on the ground. This can be true in a literal sense, as with the bridges and highway ramps that tie us into transportation networks, or the structures that are part of infrastructural systems bringing us essentials of daily life like power and water. Civic buildings play a similar role, offering access to education and the arts.

Other connections aren't as obvious: the perceptual ones forged when a building sharpens our awareness of each other, our surroundings, the past. Structures can accentuate the geography that makes San Francisco like no other metropolis, a tumble of hills and valleys between an ocean and a bay. They can also serve as perceptual links to the city that was—connections that, in turn, make us wonder what might be coming next.

CONNECTIONS

Golden Gate Bridge

If any local structure is recognized around the world, It's the span between San Francisco and the Marin Headlands erected in 1937 after decades of debate and four years of construction. This is no mere icon fashioned to launch a thousand postcards, or inspire the apocalyptic havoc delivered in such films as *It Came from Beneath the Sea*. The need for safe passage across a treacherous strait drove the design's propulsive clarity, a triumph of structural engineering and rhythmic grace that pushed the limits of what was possible for the time. The best bridges command the landscape as though they were destined to be there all along. This one does that and more, closing the gate and completing the bay. *Chief engineer, Joseph B. Strauss; length of suspension span, 1.2 miles; height of towers, 746 feet; 1937*

Dragonfly Creek Bridge

West of Upton Avenue, north of Kobbe Avenue

A half mile south of the Golden Gate is a much different span, one that conjures up a different sort of romance and, at the same time, shows San Francisco's unending capacity for surprise. A low-walled passage assembled from stacked stones behind the Presidio's Fort Scott, an obscure corner of the former military post that's now a national park, the bridge leads across a brambled, forested gully, down past a tennis court, and over the barely perceptible Dragonfly Creek. Conceived as a make-work effort to combat the Depression, the emphatic path adds order to a terrain that otherwise seems wild—a determined route with no real link to anything nearby, which adds a layer of intrigue all its own.

Believed to be constructed by the Works Progress Administration, c. 1939

485–495 Liberty Street

Even when spans of water are not involved, getting from point A to point B in a city as hilly as San Francisco can be complex. That's why the slopes are laced by hundreds of walkways, some offering shortcuts between streets and others taking the place of roads. An example of the latter is this public staircase that feels as natural as an unnatural act of construction can be. Each of the four residences along the south edge aligns horizontally to the stairs, a methodical adaptation to reality, but the overall impression is a sculpted whole, with tucked and folded cubes reminiscent of a craggy Italian townscape. Less architecture than form-making, and more memorable than if the slope had remained bare.

Gilbert Plov, 2 stories, 1941

Saint Joseph's Hospital

355 Buena Vista Avenue East

Buildings also can serve as a counterpoint to the terrain, one mass emphasizing the next. This hospital-turned-condo complex would be handsome in any neighborhood with its ruddy tile roofs and creamy stucco walls, but the way it locks into the broad flank of Buena Vista Heights gives the stocky form an almost geological presence. It's as if a cliff had been exposed and then buffed, a broad stretch of faceted rock amid houses and trees. Does the addition mar the original? Not at all. The effortlessness with which the green summit accommodates the masonry bulk accents the strength of the bedrock beneath our feet, strong enough to endure domestication as well as seismic rumbles.

Bakewell & Brown, 6 stories, 1928

750–752 Francisco Street

The most thoroughly San Franciscan connection of all is the simple thrill of a clear vast view to points beyond; in turn, that vantage point can shape a building's spirit and design. One example on Russian Hill is a duplex snug along the diagonal slope, two long, deferential volumes with spacious terraces notched into the corner of each. The materials are simple, the details plain. The real show is the panorama, a fusion of built-up city and wide-open bay echoed by terraces that are generous and intimate at once. The ease with which this simple structure folds out from its steep corner outshines contrived drama. It is intended as a perch, not a statement, and it knows better than to try and upstage what lies beyond. *Oliver Rousseau, 2 stories, 1948*

556 Commercial Street

Few spots in the Financial District cast the transportive spell of the intersection where the alleyways of Commercial and Leidesdorff streets overlap, a pair of quiet lanes tucked below the Transamerica Pyramid and other towers. Along the way are masonry buildings erected almost as soon as debris was cleared from the 1906 earthquake; most are nondescript but the one at the northeast corner is a mottled plea for attention, dusty red and yellow bricks in polychromatic lines. Throughout the city there are old buildings to admire. Rarely, though, do they come together so evocatively as to let you feel that perhaps this is how things might have been, before the modern city came along.

Charles M. Rousseau, 3 stories, 1908

The Mill Building

720 York Street

A building on its own can also strengthen the bond between then and now, serving as a reminder of the cultures that first gave it a purpose. This former wool warehouse in the northeast Mission still bears forthright lettering from an age when self-promotion was no big fuss The weathered brick walls—repaired as needed but not too much— are capped by a roof with stepped parapets like nothing else around. Commercial and residential lofts today fill the narrow block-long volume that once held craftsmen and their tools; outside are eco-friendly pavers rather than crude cobblestones. But a glimpse of olden days lingers, neighborhood roots exposed, gravitas that does not put on airs.

Laver & Curlett, restored by Pfau Long Architecture, 2 stories, 1878 and 1998

2151 Sacramento Street

A word to the wise: not all alleged connections to the past are to be believed. "This house, built in 1881, was once occupied by Sir Arthur Conan Doyle" proclaims the shiny bronze plaque on a posh confection facing Lafayette Park in Pacific Heights. In fact, the structure dates back only to 1920. Sherlock Holmes's creator may have stopped by in 1923. False facts—and icing on an architectural cake that needs no added sweetener. With a cave-like entrance below a stone balustrade, and carved lions standing guard above stained-glass family shields, this whimsy would catch the eye even without embellishments of the literary kind. *Mel Schwartz, 2 stories, 1920*

Hallidie Building

130 Sutter Street

A building with far more authoritative credentials is this filigreed stack of offices in the middle of a Financial District block. The feature known to architectural scholars is the skin, a grid of glass panes within a metal frame—or, in the words of modernist historian Kenneth Frampton, "the first application of a pure curtain wall to any building in America." Every glass-skinned tower today bears traces of that DNA, at least theoretically. By any measurement the rigor shines, especially after a painstakingly lovely restoration completed in 2013. "No age is compelled to take its beauty from preceding epochs," architect Willis Polk wrote in 1892, but we can smile at what those epochs produced.

Willis Polk, restored by McGinnis Chen Associates, 7 stories, 1918 and 2013

Sunset Branch library

1305 Eighteenth Avenue

Ascend the steps between walls inscribed with the names of respected authors. Stride through the arched loggia to the high-ceilinged circulation room inside. What you find are wooden stacks that hold books in Chinese and Russian as well as English, with computers on custom shelves at the end. This scene could not have been imagined when tycoon-turned-philanthropist Andrew Carnegie donated $750,000 to the city to expand its library system, and that's how it should be. No building type honors the goal of social equity like a public library, where people of every social class can find resources to thrive. This one still plays its part, though some names inscribed on the outer walls now draw a blank. *G. Albert Lansburgh, 1 story plus basement, 1918*

IT, IS A LAND OF HILLS AND VALLEYS, AN

* "LET THY FOUNTAINS BE *
DISPERSED ABROAD AND RIVERS
OF WATERS IN THE STREETS".

Merced Manor Reservoir

2920 Twenty-Third Avenue

Whereas buildings that facilitate infrastructure systems today tend to be mundane, designed not to look as if they cost one extra cent, in the past they were often intended as civic temples of celebration. The evidence is in this classical pump house for a 9.5-million gallon reservoir hidden beneath an asphalt cap in a residential neighborhood. As regal as a ruler's tomb, the rectangular shell is coated in oratorical quotations and ebullient moldings, swathed in an abundant green lawn. The cultural message is clear, that nature's resources exist to serve mankind. Today's environmental realities challenge that self-centered stance. But its architectural legacy remains stirring, at least in settings like this.

N. A. Eckart, San Francisco Water Department, 1 story, 1936

Richardson Apartments

365 Fulton Street

A building's outward reach can be as subtle as specific facets keyed to life on the street or the shifting city map. Here, upper floors catch the eye with a zinc prow and perforated aluminum sunscreens that slice shadows across walls of clean white and lime green—gestures meant to be seen from afar, a visual hinge between City Hall to the east and Hayes Street to the south. The sidewalk experience hones in on individual passersby, a tactile come-on where board-formed concrete columns frame the glass storefronts of the tall ground floor. In a way this is building as bridge—and an equitable bridge as well, with 120 apartments for formerly homeless people upstairs.

David Baker Architects, 5 stories, 2012

1590 Bryant Street

This literal connection has survived through neglect more than intent: an enclosed cantilevered passage that straddles a roadway and passes a post office facility on its way from one building to the next. A viaduct of sorts for a corrugated hall, it was built to transport beer from a production facility to a warehouse. After the brewery closed in the 1970s, the space became a self-storage facility until the historic shell took on a third life as a Sports Basement. What remains is the energetic incongruity of a back alley on stilts—tunneling through the air, solid form in weightless sky, an unexpected landmark by way of happenstance no planner today would allow.

Nathaniel Blaisdell, 2 stories, 1907

Bay Bridge West Approach

Beale to Fifth Streets

After the Loma Prieta earthquake in 1989, engineers determined that the western approach to the Bay Bridge needed to be rebuilt. Instead of aspiring to icon status (the quest with the new eastern span that opened in 2013), designers worked to thread safety with style through a constrained scene. The cleanly detailed concrete columns and tightly coiled ramps fuse bridge to land while navigating a path between the buildings that push close on either side. If the scenic gusto of the Golden Gate Bridge is missing, no matter. Necessity is the mother of creative engineering, and this stroke of efficient infrastructure has kinetic power all the same. *Office of Structures Design, Caltrans, 2009*

For anyone in search of clues to how to-day's city came to be, or the subterranean layers of past cultures and times, buildings can be a revelation. The moldings they wear, the forms they take, the extent to which they complement or clash with their neighbors—each of these aspects has the potential to be a story in itself, filling in the blanks and conjuring up ghosts. Location also signals more than might be obvious: structures are placed where they are for a reason, though the logic of that reason often becomes clouded with time.

Not every building or structure has these added dimensions, of course. But you come across them in more parts of town than you might think—especially in San Francisco, a city that seems to be rede-fined each generation, and where so many stories are waiting to be told.

CLUES

Vaillancourt Fountain

Justin Herman Plaza

No local piece of public art caused such uproar at its birth as this spouting provocation, which architecture critic Allan Temko famously likened to something "deposited by a giant concrete dog with square intestines." Another way to view it, now, is as a work of contextual design for a context erased. The sculpture was commissioned when the Embarcadero Freeway curved past this site on the east and north. The juts of concrete offset the decks behind; the turbulent water spilling from them masked the grind of traffic above. The defiant distraction lost its purpose when the freeway was razed in 1991, opening views to the bay—and to the fountain's drab rear, exposed to people who may not realize an elevated road was ever there.

Armand Vaillancourt, approx. 40 feet, 1971

573 South Van Ness Avenue

In certain transitory settings, a lone surviving landmark is enough to conjure up the long-gone past. This handsome Queen Anne Victorian in 1900 was the home of brewer Peter Windler, topped by a round corner tower with porthole windows. Fifty houses on its block survived the 1906 earthquake, including the even more palatial mansion of Claus Spreckels next door, but in the 1930s the area was rezoned for industrial uses. Today there's a paint store where Spreckels lived, and a gas station covers land once occupied by two-family homes. Windler's estate survives as apartments, incongruous and well kept. With the Mission District's latest renaissance, its tale most certainly is not done.

Unknown, 4 stories, 1895

255 Hyde Street

In the era before television took hold, San Francisco had more than one hundred movie houses. Thirty were on Market Street alone, and the fragile reels of recent and coming attractions needed to be stored nearby. Property owners in the Tenderloin responded by erecting film-friendly warehouses with concrete walls for climate control. One of the few remaining hints of that world is an otherwise perfunctory art moderne structure adorned at cornice level with moldings that pay homage to traditional theater masks signifying comedy and tragedy. The building now holds a homeless clinic; the masks remain above, casting their gaze but not their judgment on the often-troubled scene below. *O'Brien Brothers and W. D. Peugh, 2 stories, 1930*

Park Lane Apartments

1100 Sacramento Street

There are other ways that architectural details can recall the needs
or temper of the times in which they were conceived. That's why the
proportions are all wrong on this residential corner at the summit of
Nob Hill near Huntington Park, as if someone removed the middle
twenty floors from a building that began much taller. In fact, the top
three floors were added in 1929 to cash in on the good times about
to end. It's an ostentatious finale to an otherwise staid structure
erected just five years before, heavenly bling clashing with such stately
neighbors as the Pacific-Union Club. Jarring at the time to neighbors, no
doubt. For us, three scenic stories with the moral that booms and busts
are nothing new. *Edward E. Young, 11 stories, 1924 and 1929*

290 Lombard Street

When a building is out of scale with all others nearby, it's often because neighbors who watched it go up made sure there would be no sequel. This was the case on the north slope of Telegraph Hill after a member of the Ghirardelli family filled a lot below Coit Tower with a seven-story apartment block, a blunt presence despite corner bays and a columned entrance tailored to make stocky seem suave. Among the dismayed neighbors was architect Gardner Dailey, whose attorney suggested they demand a forty-foot height limit on future structures. The continued prominence of 290 Lombard is evidence that neighbors won the zoning battle—which means that residents of the interloper need never worry about their views being blocked. *H. C. Baumann, 7 stories, 1940*

400 Grant Avenue

We take the tourist-friendly look of Chinatown for granted, but it strikes us that way for a reason: after the 1906 earthquake, city leaders sought to banish the tight-knit ethnic community to the southern reaches of the city. In self-defense, owners of the rubbled properties rebuilt as fast and as floridly as possible. Their aim—make Chinatown a destination— worked so well that structures lacking pagodas were made-over to join the crowd. In 1924 this lodging house was recast as the Mandarin, billed as "the most elaborately decorated restaurant in America with strictly Chinese and Oriental motifs." The Mandarin is gone but the trappings remain, tribute to architecture as an act of communal self-preservation.

Joseph Cahen, Ashley & Evers, 4 stories, built 1913 and rebuilt 1924

Palace of Fine Arts

3301 Lyon Street

There's still a nostalgic glow to the 1915 Panama Pacific International Exposition, a pop-up wonderland that proclaimed the city's recovery from the 1906 earthquake. The lone piece of the fair to remain in place after that civic triumph was the gauzy landscape of a lagoon framed by classical forms, Bernard Maybeck's "point of transition from sadness to content." But the landmark we treasure today is different: the structure erected as a wooden stage set covered in glorified papier-mâché was redone in concrete in 1967 and strengthened in 2011. What endures is the aura of an immense and otherworldly realm, the shared wonder of a past that, in truth, is never as simple as it seems. *Bernard Maybeck, 158 feet to top of rotunda dome, built in 1915 and restored in 1967 and 2011*

Holy Virgin Cathedral

6210 Geary Boulevard

The diversity of urban neighborhoods is gleaned not just from census figures, but also by the physical landmarks that subcultures erect. This cathedral of the grandly named Russian Orthodox Church Outside Russia is one of only a dozen or so in the United States, an unabashed exaltation with mosaics of saints framing the entrance and five gleaming gold-leafed onion domes in the sky. It also signals the presence of a community whose members first immigrated here in the 1920s, one that has remained amid all the subsequent population shifts. Outsiders this far west on Geary are often heading somewhere else—but for a moment, they're shown that the city around us has more dimensions than we can know. *Oleg Ivanitsky, 120 feet to top of tallest cross, 1965*

Embarcadero Substation

401 Folsom Street

Buildings that serve our society, but aren't pleasant to be around, tend to be placed where not many people will notice or care. So when Pacific Gas and Electric Co. needed to add a transformer station to serve the Financial District in the 1970s, it chose a block hidden behind ramps connecting the Bay Bridge to the Embarcadero Freeway. Close enough to be useful, far enough away to be remote, the imposing box of ribbed concrete was out of sight and out of mind on the slopes of Rincon Hill… until the ramps came down and sleek housing towers started to rise. Though they crowd ever closer, the substation remains, telling of a time when downtown was where people worked but did not live.

Sidney H. Smyth Jr., 171 feet, 1973

1118 and 1122 Howard Street

Much of today's city was once bay, or mingled soil and marshes and creeks, crudely covered over to create real estate in the decades of boisterous growth that followed the Gold Rush. That doesn't mean the underlying topography is at rest, as a close look at these two otherwise nondescript buildings reveals. They were late additions to a part of town where sand was dumped atop wet earth in the 1850s, and in their nine decades of life, the humble twins have adjusted and readjusted themselves in response to slow subsidence beneath. Now they sag against each other for support, once-uniform cornice lines askew, atop a natural swale that, if it ever gets the chance, may yet return to view.

Dodge A. Reidy, 2-plus stories, 1925

Marquard's Little Cigar Store
201 O'Farrell Street

It will come as no surprise that this busy Powell Street corner once housed a newsstand, where reading materials of all sorts were sold late into the night along with liquor and various smokes. Then, after decades when most of the storefronts catered to souvenir-hunting tourists, Powell began attracting mall franchises around the same time that the Internet upended print media. In 2005, Marquard's was replaced by a chain selling logoed caps—but city planners decreed that the neon marquee should stay, "bearing witness to an important business type and signage style of a by-gone era." This it continues to do, yet it also has an air of sanctified obsolescence, more out of place each year. The relic is here. The world that gave it meaning is gone. *Arthur Lamb, 3 stories, 1907*

Doggie Diner

Sloat Boulevard and Forty-Fifth Avenue

San Francisco historic landmark #254 is a fiberglass dachshund head seven feet tall, candy apple red, mounted on a metal pole in a roadway median. It began life one block away, outside a fast-food chain that at its peak had twenty-six locations. The last Doggie Diner closed in 1986, yet this roadside attraction remained, bow-tied and inscrutable, a tribute to this transient city's love of locally sourced kitsch and supposedly simpler times. In 2000 it was moved to its current location, the closest convenient spot to its "historic" home. Official landmark status followed five years later. Forget the saying that every dog has its day; in a city that values eccentrics and where no cause is too absurd, this one looks to have as many lives as a cat. *Harold Bachman, 7 feet on pole, c. 1966*

San Francisco's waterfront in many ways is a place unto itself. State regulators have final say over much of what gets built. Nearby residents use the ballot to block projects they dislike. The port along its eastern edge, facing a protected bay, is the reason that a foggy village became one of the nation's great cities in the second half of the nineteenth century.

But this one-of-a-kind shoreline is also part and parcel of twenty-first-century San Francisco: home to all manners of architecture and activities, the outgrowth of more than 150 years of construction and revision as the need arose. If history and memories color many stops along the way, others show a city that does not want to stand still. From the edge of the ocean to the southeast corner of the city, our urban waterfront is a culmination and a work in progress—and the more firmly that it is seen as inseparable from the larger city, shaped by the same forces, the better we will understand it, and San Francisco as a whole.

WATERFRONT

Lands End Outlook

680 Point Lobos Avenue

San Francisco's best work of modern architecture since the de Young Museum is where you least expect to find it: on a tall bluff above the Pacific Ocean. The long concrete walls for this visitor center in the Golden Gate National Recreational Area emerge from landscaped dunes and extend to the walkway above the ragged ruins of Sutro Baths; the main hall stands between panels of floor-to-ceiling glass that frame the horizon for visitors approaching from the east. The design is calibrated to the setting, raw and strong to resist fog and wind. It also exudes confidence, secure in the knowledge that the shore of this peninsula is dynamic, deserving unapologetic public buildings of our time.

EHDD, 1 story, 2012

Fort Point

West end of Marine Drive

History buffs are attracted by the novelty of the westernmost of the forty-two "third style" forts built by the United States before the Civil War. The rest of us gasp at the drama of city and nature colliding with primeval force, sensations of the moment set against rock-solid remnants of the past. The masonry fortress is from the 1850s, while the airy steel bridge above was completed in 1937. Steep green slopes offset the roiled blue where ocean battles bay. The fort is focused inward on a stark terrace, not to the vistas outside. Yet this remote-seeming outpost is part of the city's daily life; ask the surfers who come for the dark silver waves, casual users of an extraordinary place. *U.S. Army Corps of Engineers, 3 stories plus rooftop designed as deck for cannon, 1853–1860*

Crissy Field

Mason Street

When the asphalt-covered supply yard of the former army post known as the Presidio was transformed into a beguiling park along the bay, a twenty-eight-acre lawn was included as a tribute to the airfield that flourished there from 1919 into the 1930s. It's an attractive oval but one that was often empty—until eight industrially scaled steel structures by Mark di Suvero were displayed there for a year by the San Francisco Museum of Modern Art. Purists were outraged! But it was a wonderful fit, artwork that tied Crissy Field to downtown's distant towers and the Golden Gate Bridge while demonstrating how our waterfront can absorb the unexpected with power and verve. *Hargreaves Associates, 100 acres, 2001. Sculptures by Mark di Suvero, painted steel, 25 to 55 feet in height, May 2013 to May 2014*

Aquatic Park Speaker Towers

Polk and Beach Streets

The urban landscape includes artifacts of technologies that otherwise are lost to time, such as these two cryptic concrete ghosts at either end of Aquatic Park. They flank the park's bathhouse and bleachers, impassive and mute, once-innovative bookends to the beachside ensemble built by the Works Progress Administration as the city's first recreational destination on the bay. The streamlined white towers held speakers to broadcast sporting events, but World War II intervened. By the time it ended, the novelty had faded—long before earbuds and mobile devices—and the towers have stood silent for decades. Now they keep watch, hinting at the civic dreams of a city that in many ways no longer exists. *William Mooser Sr. and Jr., 35 feet, 1939*

Fishermen's and Seamen's Memorial Chapel

Pier 45-B

Amid the touristic churn of Fisherman's Wharf it's easy to miss the compact wooden chapel and its bell tower at the end of a dock in the lagoon, hidden by masts that rustle with the tides. Yet it looms large in a cultural sense, built to serve the working people, often of Mediterranean descent, whose predecessors gave this harbor a reason for being before the seafood restaurants and souvenir shops. The chapel and bell tower cast their own resonant spell, spare structures framed in dark wood that stir thoughts of a different California, the deep solace of forests afar. Too much of the wharf can seem like an outdoor mall. Standing on this pier, at the chapel, all the clamor fades away. *Braccia, Heglund & Associates, 1 story, 1981, campanile by Anthony Pantaleoni added 2008*

Pier 29

The waterfront south of Fisherman's Wharf is home to the Embarcadero Historic District, lined by a row of imposing-looking piers dating back to when this was the busiest port on the West Coast. But the term *historic* can be deceptive: this pier's classical bulkhead consists of plywood coated in stucco, the replica of a 1918 structure that went up in flames in 2012. The Port of San Francisco still had the original plans on file, and rebuilding this piece of the long-gone blue-collar waterfront, albeit with different materials, was never in question. You can make a case that such gestures are deceptive—except that familiar settings enrich our mental landscape, even when the "familiar" involves some sleight of hand.

A. A. Pyle, original facade; Carey & Co., architect for restoration; 54 feet; 1918 and 2013

Ferry Building

Foot of Market Street

Conceived as the link between the self-contained peninsula and the continent beyond, this triumph of ceremonial infrastructure shows how architecture can exert a gravitational pull, anchoring Market Street to the bay where the Embarcadero's odd and even piers collide. The proud clock tower steals attention from skyscrapers twice its height, while the stacked rows of sandstone arches facing inland set a tone of compelling grandeur. No longer is this the portal for 100 million ferry riders a year; instead, the interior was redone to hold a skylit market hall that celebrates regional food and drink—and, indirectly, the ability of historic landmarks to assert themselves anew. *A. Page Brown, original architect; design team for restoration headed by SMWM; 3 stories plus 245-foot tower; 1898 and 2002*

Pier 14

Public space takes all forms, including this path into the bay that's 15 feet wide and 637 feet long. It sits atop a concrete breakwater that protects ferries from winter storms; the stroke of inspiration was to finish off the function with a narrow pedestrian corridor framed by thin rails of horizontal steel. You ascend and you depart, artistic tiles along the rails giving way to swivel chairs, and the city giving way to the bridge-pierced bay. The compression of the elongated space makes the shifting relationships of landscape more vivid the further you go. The finale is a circular landing—and views to be enjoyed as the conclusion of a journey, more rewarding than the panorama from the shore.

Port of San Francisco and Roma Design Group, 2006

Hills Plaza

345 Spear Street

Every decade, it seems, San Franciscans mobilize to prevent the erection of structures that supposedly will seal off the city from the bay. Yet such "walls" are already in place, and some of them enhance rather than detract. This block of offices and housing combines the robust forms and dappled brown brick of the historic Hills Bros. coffee plant with a broad wing that, though taller and of similar materials, is designed to let the original's arched vigor take center stage. It's a blend of old and new that is comfortable without feeling false, now serving as a transition between the Embarcadero and the glass high-rises of Rincon Hill. A wall that's not a wall, but a binding force instead. *George Kelham, Whisler-Patri, 19 stories, 1924 and 1986*

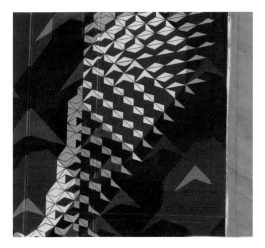

Bayview Rise

Pier 92

In a city where public murals are commonplace, only one cloaks the west wall of a derelict grain silo with geometric flurries of blue, red, yellow, green, and pink. Floodlit at night for greater effect, the artistic ascension has quickly become a visual icon along Islais Creek, marking the northern entrance to a neighborhood in physical and cultural flux. Though some of the imagery makes reference to local history, what's striking is the overall spectacle and size, amplified by the juxtaposition of lustrous paint against scarred concrete. Like all of San Francisco, the waterfront is a place of contrasts—a place where audacious acts of the imagination can be the most satisfying alterations of all. *Mural by artists Laura Haddad and Tom Drugan, painted by R. B. Morris III, 197 feet by 72 feet, 2014*

ACKNOWLEDGMENTS

A city is enriched by the cumulative value of its buildings and their creators. A book about a city's buildings is a cumulative effort as well.

The first round of thanks goes to my *Chronicle* readers, who feel a stubborn passion for the city around them and are eager to suggest buildings that might deserve attention, several of which are found in these pages. Equally valuable are the scholars and planners eager to assist a reporter who needs help on deadline, filling in such essential details as who an architect might have been and when a building might have risen. This isn't as simple as you think—it doesn't help that our 1906 earthquake destroyed city records—so I am grateful to such founts of knowledge as Mary Brown of the San Francisco Planning Department, architectural historian Gary Goss, and ever-resourceful Christopher VerPlanck.

Heyday is a regional treasure all its own, and I'm flattered that it has allowed me again to put my visceral affection for San Francisco into photographs and words. Malcolm Margolin is a beneficent guru, Gayle Wattawa and Molly Woodward the most discreetly (and rightly) demanding of editors. George Young has been a tireless, welcome champion from the start. As for art director Diane Lee and designer Rebecca LeGates, it's a revelation to see what they find within the photographs I send their way.

Finally, I'm lucky to be employed by a newspaper where so many coworkers care so much about their surroundings. Reporters like David Perlman and Carl Nolte are Bay Area treasures as well as great fun to work with. Managing editor Audrey Cooper gives neighborhood walking tours in her free time. Mark Lundgren not only keeps my copy in line but spends weekends as one of the volunteers who have labored to help make the Presidio the varied green jewel that it is. Danielle Mollette-Parks lays out my weekly column with an architectural savvy that testifies to her years in Chicago. Fellow reporter Peter Hartlaub has won me over on the merits of Sutro Tower, while J. K. Dineen knows more about what's up next than anyone around. The list could go on; in this age of single-issue advocacy and preordained points of view, the *Chronicle* has a staff of smart people who love this remarkable region but look at it with questioning eyes. As should we all.

ABOUT THE AUTHOR

John King is the *San Francisco Chronicle's* Urban Design Critic and author of the 2011 Heyday book *Cityscapes: San Francisco and Its Buildings.* He joined the paper in 1992 and has been in his current post since 2001. An honorary member of the American Society of Landscape Architects and 2013 Recipient of the International Journalism Award from Lambda Alpha International, he has been honored for his work by groups including the California Preservation Foundation and the California chapter of the American Institute of Architects. He lives in Berkeley with his wife and daughter.

HEYDAY
into California

About Heyday

Heyday is an independent, nonprofit publisher and unique cultural institution. We promote widespread awareness and celebration of California's many cultures, landscapes, and boundary-breaking ideas. Through our well-crafted books, public events, and innovative outreach programs we are building a vibrant community of readers, writers, and thinkers.

Thank You

It takes the collective effort of many to create a thriving literary culture. We are thankful to all the thoughtful people we have the privilege to engage with. Cheers to our writers, artists, editors, storytellers, designers, printers, bookstores, critics, cultural organizations, readers, and book lovers everywhere!

We are especially grateful for the generous funding we've received for our publications and programs during the past year from foundations and hundreds of individual donors. Major supporters include:

Alliance for California Traditional Arts; Anonymous (6); Arkay Foundation; Judith and Phillip Auth; Judy Avery; Carol Baird and Alan Harper; Paul Bancroft III; The Bancroft Library; Richard and Rickie Ann Baum; BayTree Fund; S. D. Bechtel, Jr. Foundation; Jean and Fred Berensmeier; Berkeley Civic Arts Program and Civic Arts Commission; Joan Berman; Nancy Bertelsen; Barbara Boucke; Beatrice Bowles, in memory of Susan S. Lake; John Briscoe; David Brower Center; Lewis and Sheana Butler; Helen Cagampang; California Historical Society; California Indian Heritage Center Foundation; California State Parks Foundation; Joanne Campbell; The Campbell Foundation; James and Margaret Chapin; Graham Chisholm; The Christensen Fund; Jon Christensen; Cynthia Clarke; Community Futures Collective; Compton Foundation; Lawrence Crooks; Lauren and Alan Dachs; Nik Dehejia; Topher Delaney; Chris Desser and Kirk Marckwald; Lokelani Devone; Frances Dinkelspiel and Gary Wayne; Doune Fund; The Durfee Foundation; Megan Fletcher and J.K. Dineen; Michael Eaton and Charity Kenyon; Richard and Gretchen Evans; Flow Fund Circle; Friends of the Roseville Library; Furthur Foundation; The Wallace Alexander Gerbode Foundation; Patrick Golden; Nicola W. Gordon; Wanda Lee Graves and Stephen Duscha; The Walter and Elise Haas

Fund; Coke and James Hallowell; Theresa Harlan and Ken Tiger; Cindy Heitzman; Carla Hills; Sandra and Charles Hobson; Nettie Hoge; Donna Ewald Huggins; JiJi Foundation; Claudia Jurmain; Kalliopeia Foundation; TK/CROUL Marty and Pamela Krasney; Robert and Karen Kustel; Guy Lampard and Suzanne Badenhoop; Thomas Lockard and Alix Marduel; Thomas J. Long Foundation; Bryce Lundberg; Sam and Alfreda Maloof Foundation for Arts & Crafts; Michael McCone; Giles W. and Elise G. Mead Foundation; Moore Family Foundation; Michael J. Moratto, in memory of Major J. Moratto; Stewart R. Mott Foundation; The MSB Charitable Fund; Karen and Thomas Mulvaney; Richard Nagler; National Wildlife Federation; Native Arts and Cultures Foundation; Humboldt Area Foundation, Native Cultures Fund; The Nature Conservancy; Nightingale Family Foundation; Steven Nightingale and Lucy Blake; Northern California Water Association; Ohlone-Costanoan Esselen Nation; Panta Rhea Foundation; David Plant; Jean Pokorny; Steven Rasmussen and Felicia Woytak; Restore Hetch Hetchy; Robin Ridder; Spreck and Isabella Rosekrans; Alan Rosenus; The San Francisco Foundation; Toby and Sheila Schwartzburg; Sierra College; Stephen M. Silberstein Foundation; Ernest and June Siva, in honor of the Dorothy Ramon Learning Center; Carla Soracco; John and Beverly Stauffer Foundation; Radha Stern, in honor of Malcolm Margolin and Diane Lee; Roselyne Chroman Swig; TomKat Charitable Trust; Tides Foundation; Sonia Torres; Michael and Shirley Traynor; The Roger J. and Madeleine Traynor Foundation; Lisa Van Cleef and Mark Gunson; Patricia Wakida; John Wiley & Sons, Inc.; Peter Booth Wiley and Valerie Barth; Bobby Winston; Dean Witter Foundation; Yocha Dehe Wintun Nation; and Yosemite Conservancy.

Board of Directors

Getting Involved

To learn more about our publications, events, membership club, and other ways you can participate, please visit www.heydaybooks.com.